NATIONAL GEOGRAPHIC

Ladders

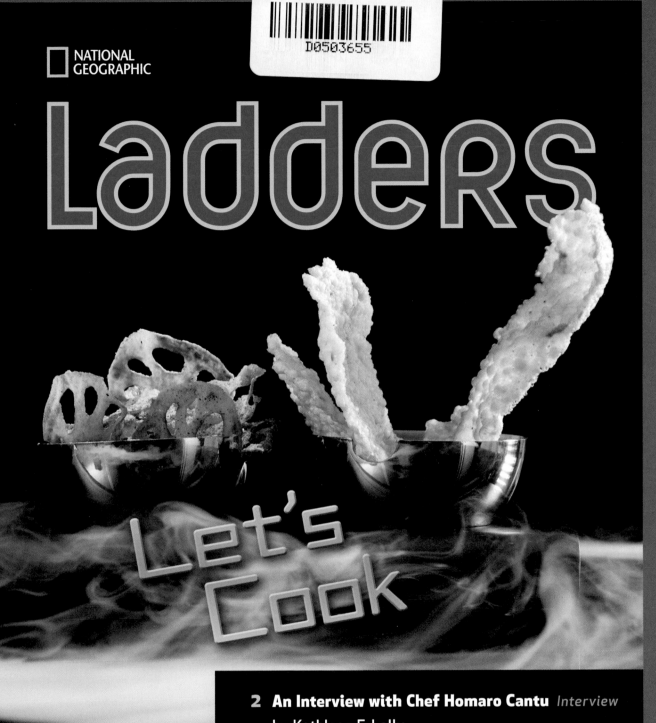

Let's Cook

An Interview with CHEF HOMARO CANTU

by Kathleen F. Lally

Homaro Cantu is a chef. He owns two restaurants in Chicago, Illinois. He has found new ways to prepare food. He changes its look, taste, and texture. Texture is how something feels. He is using science and technology to change our ideas about food. His ideas may change how people eat in the future.

National Geographic: Good afternoon, Chef Cantu. Can you please explain what **molecular gastronomy** is?

Chef Cantu: Molecular gastronomy involves exploring the science behind traditional cooking methods. A molecular gastronomist is a chef who explores the world of science and food. This new kind of chef works in a professional kitchen, experimenting with science and art and melding them together.

NG: How did you learn to do what you do?

Chef Cantu: I have been working at this for a long time. What I know really comes from a lot of practice. I start with the fundamentals on how food usually is prepared, and then I branch off into more creative directions.

National Geographic: How do you get ideas about what kinds of foods to develop?

Chef Cantu: I get ideas from all over the place. I think about the foods that you know and love, and then I make these foods out of other foods that are healthier for you. To create innovative foods, I use modern technology and tools such as lasers and machines that produce sound waves. I experiment and I mix foods together in different ways. I combine flavors, temperatures, and textures in unusual ways. I create foods that might seem impossible to make.

∧ High tech tools surround Chef Cantu. He uses them to prepare foods in new ways.

NG: What are some foods you have developed that might be of particular interest to students?

Chef Cantu: I played around with the idea of creating juices without packages. I can take an orange, apply sound waves to it, and the sound waves liquefy the orange from the inside out. The seeds, the pulp, and the tissue that lines the skin changes from solid to liquid. Now I've got orange juice in an orange. The orange juice producers would not need cartons. They would not add sugar or chemicals.

National Geographic: Do your family and friends ever affect what you discover?

Chef Cantu: Yes. In fact I have a very interesting example. I have a friend who was undergoing medical treatments, and the treatments made food taste bad to her. She asked me if I could create something that would help. My staff and I tested thousands of ingredients. We found a berry that helped eliminate the bad taste. People call it the miracle berry. Now many people are using this berry to help them when they have difficulty with their sense of taste, but the berry has an unexpected effect on those with a normal sense of taste.

NG: How does the berry work?

Chef Cantu: It basically blocks the sour receptors on the tongue. For my friend it made food taste normal, but for others it has an interesting effect. I will give you a demonstration.

1.

Taste the crushed tablet that was made from the miracle berry.

∧ The miracle berry grows in Africa. After eating it, sour foods taste sweet.

2.

Now taste the lemon. It will taste like lemonade. Next, taste the lime. The lime will taste like an orange.

∧ The chemical from the berry makes a sour lemon taste like sweet lemonade.

∧ The chemical makes a sour lime taste like sweet orange juice.

3.

Squeeze lemon into club soda. This is a **solution** of water, **carbon dioxide,** and lemon juice. That's it. But it tastes like a sweet soda—as if you had stirred sugar into the solution.

∨ No sugar is needed to make this fizzy drink taste sweet.

National Geographic: Where do you get the ingredients you use for cooking?

Chef Cantu: I get my ingredients mostly from local farms. If I can't get them locally, my staff and I try to grow them ourselves. If that's not possible, then I can find the ingredients some place else because I have a very wide network of sources.

NG: Where is it that you grow your own ingredients?

Chef Cantu: My restaurant has a room in which my staff and I grow plants using a technique called **aeroponics.** The plants are grown without the use of soil. Water with all needed nutrients is sprayed onto the roots of the plants. The nutrients come from compost made using food scraps from the restaurant. The aeroponics room has the right amount of humidity, heat, light, and carbon dioxide—everything needed to grow plants perfectly. It makes a lot of sense to have this room located right on the lower level of the restaurant. The plants are grown and used in the same location, so there is no need to transport the plants from one location to another.

> ∧ Chef Cantu believes food should look as good as it tastes. In this kitchen, he shows how one treat is prepared.

∨ **Colorful cuisine**

∨ **Savory snowmen**

National Geographic: Can you please explain more about how you are focusing on health issues?

Chef Cantu: I am focusing on addressing health problems such as obesity and diabetes. I am trying to help solve these problems by making fun food products. The demand for junk foods and foods with sugar is never going to go away. What I can do is replace sugar with materials that taste sweet but really do not have any sugar. I replace the "junk" in junk food with healthful foods that taste like junk foods. This is one way I approach food from a different perspective.

NG: What advice would you give a student who is interested in food science?

Chef Cantu: I would suggest entering science competitions. Those experiences may help show a student how much he or she needs to learn within the field. I also think it is important to get an idea of what it is like to work in food science— maybe spend a day with a scientist from a university, or talk to a chef about how he or she uses food science every day.

∨ Fun fungi

Check In How might Chef Cantu's foods help people?

Food Magic

by Glen Phelan

This seafood feast was prepared using the science of molecular gastronomy. It includes several products from the sea.

Food should look as good as it tastes and taste as good as it looks. The meal in this photo is perfect for seafood lovers. It includes mussels, scallops, clams, and crabs. The foods were prepared using **molecular gastronomy** so that the textures, colors, and flavors blend well. The plate looks a bit like the seashore. The "sand" is made from seaweed, bread crumbs, and other ingredients. The "sea foam" is a **mixture** of clam juice, celery, garlic, and onions. The "beach plants" are a kind of chive.

Unexpected sights, textures, and tastes are part of molecular gastronomy. Don't let the fancy name scare you, though, because you don't need a high-tech kitchen to join the fun. Many cooks are using molecular gastronomy methods at home. You can find most of the equipment in specialty shops. People even share molecular gastronomy recipes online.

Read the recipes on the next pages. They show how different cooking methods can change the properties of food.

Spheres

Chefs make **spheres** to change the look and taste of foods. A sphere is shaped like a ball. The spheres in the picture hold fruit juice. When you bite them, they burst with flavor.

Chefs can turn liquids into spheres. They mix the liquid with sodium alginate. This natural chemical comes from seaweed. It dissolves in the liquid and makes a **solution.** Chefs drop this solution into another solution that has calcium. A thin skin forms around each drop. The drops form spheres. The spheres can be made as small as peas or much larger.

Chefs use molecular gastronomy to make spheres and other foods. The recipes for these foods call for exact measurements. So the chefs use special scales that can measure fractions of a gram!

Cantaloupe Juice Spheres

- 3 g $\left(\frac{1}{9} \text{ oz}\right)$ calcium chloride
- 480 mL (2 cups) water
- 3 g $\left(\frac{1}{9} \text{ oz}\right)$ sodium alginate
- 240 mL (1 cup) cantaloupe juice

1. Stir the calcium chloride and the water in a bowl. The calcium chloride will dissolve. Place the solution in the refrigerator for 15 to 30 minutes.

2. Meanwhile, dissolve the sodium alginate in one-third of the cantaloupe juice. Then add the rest of the juice.

3. Take the calcium chloride solution out of the refrigerator. Drop the juice solution into the calcium chloride solution with a dropper. The drops will become spheres as they sink.

4. Leave the spheres in the calcium chloride solution for about 1 minute. Then use a slotted spoon to remove the spheres. Rinse the spheres in plain water and serve.

These cantaloupe juice spheres have a light, delicious flavor.

Gels

Some foods are gels. A **gel** is a mixture of a solid and a liquid. Orange gelatin is a gel. The long noodle in the picture is also a gel.

To make a gel, you need a gelling agent. A gelling agent helps a mixture form a gel. Agar is a gelling agent that comes from seaweed. Agar helps a gel stay firm even at high temperatures. So gels made with agar can be served hot.

The single piece of spaghetti in the photo is 1 meter (about 3 feet) long.

Arugula Spaghetti

- 480 mL (2 cups) fresh arugula
- 160 mL ($\frac{2}{3}$ cup) water
- 3 g agar ($\frac{1}{9}$ oz)

1. First, mix the water and arugula in a blender. Arugula is a type of salad leaf. Blending creates a smooth mixture.

2. Next, pour the mixture into a pan and stir in the agar. Bring the mixture to a boil. Turn off the heat.

3. Then, fill a kitchen syringe with the mixture. Squirt the mixture into a long plastic tube. Place the tube in cold water and wait while the gel forms.

4. Finally, push air into the tube with the empty syringe. An arugula noodle will come out. Enjoy this new way of eating salad!

Edible Menu

You are at one of Chef Cantu's restaurants for dinner. What's the first course? The menu! Yes, you eat the menu.

Chef Cantu makes the menus out of materials you can eat. He then uses inks made from juices to print on them. The menus can be frozen, baked, or fried. Chef Cantu can make a menu taste like almost anything.

Look at the menu. Not only are the listed foods delicious, the menu is too. It's edible!

Why make a menu that you can eat? Chef Cantu wants to help the environment. Every year, restaurants use large amounts of paper for menus. Chef Cantu's menus cut waste and save trees.

Chef Cantu always thinks about food in new ways. He is sure that his big ideas will lead to a better future.

Check In Which of the foods described in this piece would you most like to try?

Temperature TECH

by Tom Wickland

It seems like magic. You pour cold lemonade into the container and screw on the cap. Two hours later, the lemonade is still cold! Another day, you pour hot soup into the container and take it to school. At lunchtime, the soup is still hot! This container that keeps cold things cold and hot things hot is a **thermos.**

In the 1890s, James Dewar invented the thermos. He studied how temperature affects gases. He cooled hydrogen gas to a very low temperature. That changed it from a gas to a liquid.

Dewar needed a way to keep cold liquids cold. If the liquid warmed up, it would change back to a gas. He made a glass ball with an inner wall and an outer wall. There was nothing between the walls. The space between them was a **vacuum.** The vacuum helped keep heat from moving, so very little heat could enter his container. The hydrogen could stay liquid for a long time.

A modern thermos works like Dewar's container. A modern thermos is shaped like a cylinder. It is usually made of metal or plastic. These materials don't break as easily as glass.

∧ **Modern thermos**

James Dewar holds an early thermos, a device he invented to store very cold liquids.

Cool It!

Dewar also worked with nitrogen. This gas makes up most of the air we breathe. Gases are made of particles that zip past each other and spread out. When gases cool, the particles slow down. Dewar cooled nitrogen to a very low temperature. Its particles slowed down, came together, and formed a liquid.

Executive Chef Ben Roche uses **molecular gastronomy.** He studies how temperature affects foods. Here he is about to place a soft banana in liquid nitrogen.

The banana starts to get very cold and hard. Its properties are changing.

The brittle banana shatters when it hits the hard surface. As the pieces of banana warm up, their properties change again. The pieces become soft.

Chefs use liquid nitrogen to cool foods quickly. A container of warm broth can take 15 minutes to cool in a bowl of ice. But liquid nitrogen can cool it in seconds. Liquid nitrogen can also change foods in other ways. The pictures show how it changes a banana.

Chef Roche removes the banana from the liquid nitrogen. The banana is now very cold, very hard, and very brittle.

Chef Roche drops the banana onto a hard surface.

Heat It!

Have you heard of hot pot cooking? One legend says it started centuries ago in East Asia. Mongol warriors put water and food in their round helmets. Then they set the helmets in the hot embers of a campfire. Soup anyone?

People still enjoy cooking a meal in this simple way. You place a pot of broth on a hot plate on the table. Turn the hot plate up high until the liquid boils. Then turn the heat down. Keep the temperature just below boiling while the broth simmers.

Now the fun begins. People at the table add different foods. Foods that need to cook longer are added first. They might include meats, fish, or shellfish. Tofu, noodles, eggs, and vegetables may also be added. When the **mixture** is cooked, use chopsticks to take out what you like. Then dip it in sauce and eat it hot.

There's no rush with hot pot cooking. A meal can take hours as people tell stories around the table.

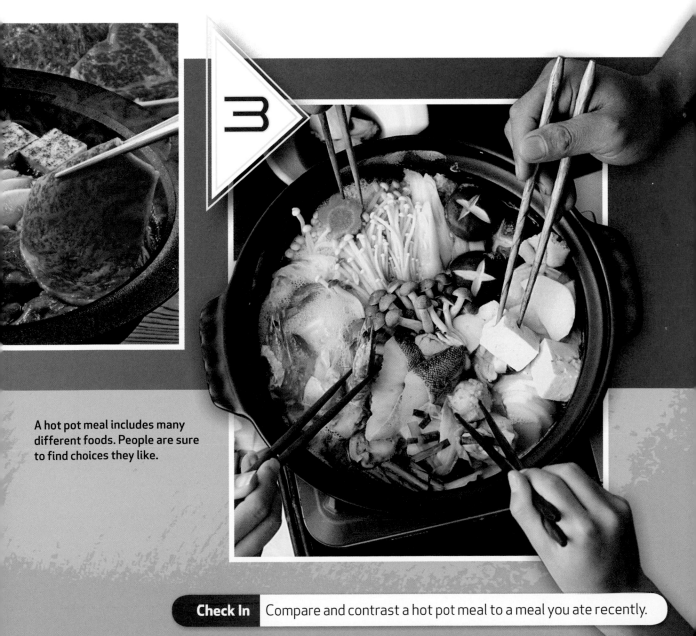

A hot pot meal includes many different foods. People are sure to find choices they like.

Check In Compare and contrast a hot pot meal to a meal you ate recently.

How to Make fizz

by Jennifer K. Cocson

Have you ever made ice cream? You can use a machine to make the creamy **mixture.** These machines are good—but expensive. You can also make ice cream with what you may have in your kitchen. Look at the items on these two pages. They are easy to find, except the fizzy granules.

What You Need

1 cup whole milk

3 quarts crushed ice

$\frac{3}{4}$ cup water

1 cup whipping cream

2 cups table salt

8 teaspoons fizzy granules

$\frac{1}{4}$ cup sugar

$\frac{1}{2}$ teaspoon vanilla extract

Ice Cream

Fizzy granules are sometimes called popping rocks. They are sold in some stores. An adult can find them online. They have tiny pockets of trapped **carbon dioxide** gas. Carbon dioxide makes soft drinks fizzy. When the granules dissolve in your mouth or are bitten, the carbon dioxide escapes with a little "pop" or "fizz." This can jazz up your ice cream.

1 pair
oven mitts

4 bowls and 4 spoons

2 feet
duct tape

1 mixing spoon

1 gallon
freezer bag

1 quart
freezer bag

1

Pour the milk, whipping cream, sugar, and vanilla extract into
the quart-size bag. Mix everything together with a spoon.
Squeeze out all of the air from the bag and seal the bag
tightly. For extra protection, double seal the bag using
a strip of duct tape along the sealed edge.

2

Place the quart-size bag into a gallon-size bag. Pack ice around the small bag. Then pour the salt and water over the ice. Squeeze out all of the air from the large bag and seal it tightly. Double seal it using a strip of duct tape along the sealed edge.

What Ice and Salt Do

What happens to an ice cube in your hand? Energy from your warm hand moves into the cold ice. This cools your hand. It melts the ice. The same thing happens with the mixture in the bag. Energy moves from the creamy mixture into the cold ice and water. The creamy mixture gets cold. But why add salt?

Adding salt makes the ice and water mixture get very cold. It gets even colder than it would without the salt. This makes the creamy mixture very cold.

3

Carefully rock the bags back and forth in your hands, using oven mitts to protect your hands from the cold. Keep moving the bags around until the mixture in the small bag has frozen into a soft solid.

What Mixing Does

Ice crystals form inside the creamy mixture as it cools and freezes. Some of the crystals can grow larger than others, giving the mixture a rough, icy texture. Moving the bag around breaks up the larger crystals, resulting in a smoother texture.

After about 15 minutes, open the large bag, and pull out the small bag. Discard the large bag, ice, and salty water. Rinse the outside of the small bag to get rid of any remaining salt. Open the bag, scoop out the ice cream into serving bowls, and sprinkle the ice cream with fizzy granules. Grab a spoon and enjoy ice cream that bubbles on your tongue!

Think about how you made ice cream. Compare how the solid ice and the creamy liquid mixture changed. Now enjoy your ice cream!

Check In Compare fizzy ice cream to regular ice cream.

Discuss

1. Think about the four pieces in this book. Explain the role that science plays in food preparation in each piece.

2. Arugula spaghetti is a delicious gel. Compare and contrast a gel to a solid and liquid.

3. Liquid nitrogen changed the banana. Predict how cooling a flower in this way might affect its properties.

4. From different pieces in this book, pick two mixtures. Describe how their properties are similar and how they are different.

5. What else would you like to learn about how foods can be prepared?